PENGUIN BOOKS
EXAM WARRIORS

Narendra Modi serves as the Prime Minister of India, the world's largest democracy. He has been Prime Minister since May 2014, after leading his party to the first full parliamentary majority government in India in three decades. His victory was propelled by historic support from India's youth, particularly first-time voters.

As Prime Minister, Modi has presided over transformative economic and social sector reforms, which have given a strong boost to India's development journey.

The education sector has been particularly close to Modi's heart. He is an inspirational leader for the youth. His monthly radio programme, 'Mann Ki Baat', is extremely popular among all sections of society. It was in this programme that he addressed Exam Warriors, first in 2015 and then subsequently in 2016 and 2017.

Previously, Modi served as the Chief Minister of Gujarat from 2001 to 2014. He has also held key organizational responsibilities in the Bharatiya Janata Party, including that of the General Secretary (Organization).

Modi enjoys reading, writing and interacting with people. He is among the most followed leaders on social media, which he uses regularly. He also connects with people across the world through his own app, the Narendra Modi Mobile App.

EXAM WARRIORS

NARENDRA MODI

PENGUIN BOOKS

An imprint of Penguin Random House

PENGUIN BOOKS

USA | Canada | UK | Ireland | Australia
New Zealand | India | South Africa | China

Penguin Books is part of the Penguin Random House group of companies
whose addresses can be found at global.penguinrandomhouse.com

Published by Penguin Random House India Pvt. Ltd
7th Floor, Infinity Tower C, DLF Cyber City,
Gurgaon 122 002, Haryana, India

First published in Penguin Books by Penguin Random House India 2018

Copyright © Narendra Modi 2018

Technology and knowledge partner BlueKraft Digital Foundation

Concept and character design copyright © Bombay Design House 2018

ISBN 9780143441502

Typeset in Kidprint MT Std by Manipal Digital Systems, Manipal
Printed at Replika Press Pvt. Ltd, India

www.penguin.co.in

CONTENTS

A NOTE FROM THE AUTHOR ix

MANTRA 1
Exams Are Like Festivals—Celebrate Them! 1

MANTRA 2
Exams Test Your Current Preparation, Not You. Chill! 7

MANTRA 3
Laugh In, Laugh Out 11

MANTRA 4
Be a Warrior, Not a Worrier! 17

MANTRA 5
Knowledge Is Permanent—Pursue It 23

MANTRA 6
Compete—with Yourself 27

MANTRA 7
It's Your Time—Make the Most of It 31

MANTRA 8
The Present Is God's Greatest 'Present'—Live Here and Now 37

MANTRA 9
Technology Is a Great Teacher—Embrace It 43

MANTRA 10
To Do Your Best, Take Adequate Rest 49

MANTRA 11
Sleep Is a Great Weapon—Sharpen It 53

MANTRA 12
Play to Shine 57

MANTRA 13
Be Your Own Anchor—Celebrate Your Strengths
61

MANTRA 14
Revise and Become Wise
65

MANTRA 15
Little Things Matter—Observe Exam Discipline
73

MANTRA 16
Your Exam, Your Methods—Choose Your Own Style
77

MANTRA 17
Presentation Is Key—Master It
81

MANTRA 18
To Cheat Is to Be Cheap
87

MANTRA 19
The Answer Sheet Is a One-Way Ticket—Move Ahead
91

MANTRA 20
Discover Yourself—Experience All That Life Offers
97

MANTRA 21
India Is Incredible—Travel and Explore
101

MANTRA 22
As One Journey Ends, Another Begins
107

MANTRA 23
Aspire, Not to Be, but to Do
113

MANTRA 24
Be Grateful
117

MANTRA 25
Yoga Brings Transformation—Practise Regularly
123

LETTERS TO PARENTS AND TEACHERS
127

YOGASANAS
133–172

Dedicated to
the youth of New India

A Note from the Author

India is the world's most youthful nation, with two-thirds of our population under the age of thirty-five. Young Indians have distinguished themselves in a wide range of fields not only in India but also overseas. It is the strength and skills of these youngsters that will usher in a New India.

Interacting with the youth is something I have always enjoyed. That is why, in February 2015, I decided to devote that month's 'Mann Ki Baat' programme to students appearing for their board examinations. In India, these exams are typically held around late February and early March. 'Mann Ki Baat', I thought, could be a wonderful medium to talk directly to students who were appearing for the exams and support them during this crucial phase of their lives.

It was an experiment of sorts and the end result was very encouraging. The response to that particular 'Mann Ki Baat' was overwhelming. Before the programme, several students from all over India shared their thoughts through letters, emails and MyGov. Parents and teachers wrote congratulatory messages to me for taking up an issue that deserved attention.

After the Class X and XII results were published later in the year, students wrote in to say that the 'Mann Ki Baat' episode had helped them immensely in their preparation, reducing their pre-exam stress. In fact, a parent wrote to me saying, 'Modiji, one of my children appeared for the Class XII exam and the other for Class X. They were tremendously nervous but your "Mann Ki Baat" had an effect on them that even our words did not.' Such letters really touched me and thus it was decided to once again address exam students, their parents and teachers in the corresponding months of 2016 as well as 2017.

The experience of these three 'Mann Ki Baat' episodes and the responses received convinced me that I should compile the various themes discussed in them into a book.

This book is for all students who are appearing for examinations. They are the 'Exam Warriors'—brave youngsters taking part in the festival of exams. The book drives home the important point that when it comes to examinations, there is no need to worry excessively or view it as a life-and-death situation.

The book seeks to add to the debate and discourse around the importance of stress-free examinations and the need to pursue knowledge over marks. It aims to be a catalyst that will trigger discussions whose ultimate beneficiaries will be our Exam Warriors. The more we talk about these issues, share our views and experiences and learn from others, the greater will be the chances of ensuring that our children have the fun-filled childhood that they deserve. It is our collective duty to ensure that their childhood is not overshadowed by the burden of exams and the constant anxiety of 'What do I do next?'

In the spirit of continuing dialogue, this book contains activities that are fun and thought-provoking. On some pages, students can even write their own Mantras to motivate fellow Exam Warriors.

A series of asanas and breathing exercises are also included in this book. Exam Warriors should make yoga a part of their lives. From overcoming stress to becoming fitter, the advantages of practising yoga are manifold.

Being a firm believer in the power of technology, I have integrated this book with the Narendra Modi Mobile App. After all, it is all about sharing and growing—Exam Warriors can share their exam journeys with others and discover how others have embarked on theirs, through the app.

I have also written about other aspects, such as why one must always pursue one's passion, try to discover oneself, and why youngsters must play, travel extensively and devote some time in the service of society. 'Smaller' but equally important areas of exam discipline and the significance of presentation have also been covered in the book.

No exam journey is complete without the support of parents and teachers. I have written to them as well, thanking them for the crucial role they play and seeking their continued support in encouraging our Exam Warriors.

Numerous inputs from students, parents and teachers before 'Mann Ki Baat' and the many letters that poured in after the examination season were particularly useful while writing this book.

I hope you enjoy reading *Exam Warriors* as much as I enjoyed writing it. Feedback and more ideas on the questions raised in this book are welcome.

Happy reading!

All the best for the exams!

नरेन्द्र मोदी

Narendra Modi
26 January 2018

How to Use the Book

- This book is a unique experience which can be enjoyed not only by reading it but also by engaging with the Exam Warrior Community through the Narendra Modi Mobile App.

- The book stresses on 'doing and developing'—when you learn a concept, you can understand it fully through practice. In this spirit, there are enjoyable and creative activities after every Mantra in the book.

- Share and grow—Knowledge, when shared, multiplies. Most activities can be shared on the Exam Warrior Community page. You can exchange learnings and views with other Exam Warriors, and grow together.

- The Exam Warrior Community page also enables you to share your achievements and any other content with friends, family and teachers.

- In the course of reading the Mantras, Exam Warriors will surely have lots to express. Periodically in the book there are 'My Mantra' pages where Exam Warriors can pen their own Mantras that can be shared on the Narendra Modi Mobile App, which others can read and draw inspiration from.

- This book is like your personal diary! You can note down your thoughts, prepare your own timetable and do much more. Writing in the book is best done with a pencil or ballpoint pen.

- You will find a repository of information on yogasanas and breathing exercises which can be used not only while preparing for exams but also for life. The guidance of yoga teachers can be valuable in this regard.

Good luck, Exam Warriors!

1

"

Exams Are Like Festivals—
Celebrate Them!

"

Exams Are Like Festivals—Celebrate Them!

The closest parallel to exams is festivals!

You may be surprised but let me explain why . . .

To begin with, there is a great spirit of anticipation in the run-up to festivals. They are among the most awaited events of the year. I am sure you look forward to festivals such as Holi, Diwali, Eid, Christmas and Guru Purab. Similarly, haven't you been discussing your exams months in advance and planning for them diligently?

Festivals bring out the best in us. Exams too are meant to bring out the best in you. The year-long acquisition of knowledge and thorough preparation strengthen you.

Festivals are best enjoyed together. The more people you celebrate festivals with, the happier you feel.

Even in the case of exams, you are not celebrating this festival alone. Lakhs of students—from Kashmir to Kanyakumari, from Kutch to Kohima—are celebrating with you. You also have the support of your family and friends.

It is believed that prayers during festivals are more rewarding. Similarly, studying before and during exams is more effective. ☺

I am confident that you are all set to celebrate the festival of exams with much cheer and happiness.

ACTIVITY I: Holi spreads cheer and forgiveness.
Makar Sankranti shows a deep bond with nature.
Raksha Bandhan celebrates relationships.
Festivals that entail fasts inculcate will power
and determination.
Each festival brings out something valuable.
Likewise, what do exams bring out in you?

ACTIVITY II: Draw a scene depicting your favourite festival.

Scan the QR code and upload your drawing. Invite other Exam Warriors to join your celebrations.

MY MANTRA

2

"

Exams Test
Your Current
Preparation,
Not You.
Chill!

"

Exams Test Your Current Preparation, Not You. Chill!

In this hyper-competitive era of relentless pressure from all sides, it is easy to think that exams are a matter of life and death, and that failure is final. But exams are not about life and death. Do not get bogged down by any pressure, particularly the fear of failure.

Who can forget our erstwhile President Dr A.P.J. Abdul Kalam!

Do you know something interesting about him? He originally wanted to become a fighter pilot but narrowly missed the opportunity. Yet he did not remain perpetually dejected. Instead he became the great scientist we remember him as today. How different the Indian nuclear programme would be if it were not for him!

What does this instance illustrate? **That one particular test or exam cannot define a person. Life is so much more than that.**

Setbacks, if any, must not deter you from pursuing your dreams. Life is about opportunities to reflect, learn and script new stories of success.

Exams are just one of the many important events in life, not the *only* one. Can one exam be the *sole* factor in determining one's excellence and true potential? Certainly not.

Placing examinations in the larger context of life and not in absolute terms is the secret to burden-free and satisfying preparations.

Prepare, appear and do not fear failure.

ACTIVITY: Write a letter addressed to your exam, stating why you are not scared of it.

DEAR EXAM,

I'M NOT SCARED OF YOU BECAUSE . . .

EXAM WARRIORS

FROM: _____

© Exam Warriors

Scan the QR code to post your letter. It may inspire others too!

3

"

Laugh In,
Laugh Out

"

Laugh In, Laugh Out

Yes, you read that right. ☺

Laugh your way into the exam hall and laugh out of it.

Prepare for exams with a smile, carry the same smile all the way into the exam hall, and out of it. Even if you do not feel like it, SMILE.

Smiling fosters relaxation. With greater relaxation comes greater ability to recall.

As a student, I was sometimes in situations where I couldn't recall an answer during the exam. However, after the exam ended, the answer struck me within minutes. This may have happened to many people.

Later on, I realized this was because I felt relaxed once the exam was over and could remember the answer with ease.

You may not give your *best* when you're under stress because your knowledge takes a back seat and pressure drives you. Do you want to be controlled by unnecessary pressure or would you rather control the pressure?

The choice is obvious . . .

A relaxed mind is the secret to success, not only in an examination hall but in life as well.

Always remember: relax to recall.

Enter the exam hall with a smile, answer with ease and leave with an even bigger smile!

ACTIVITY I: Fill and send the 'Laugh Hard Card' to your best friend.

Find the tearaway 'Laugh Hard Card' on Page 179.

Scan the QR code to download more 'LAUGH HARD CARDS'. Share more laughs with your friends.

ACTIVITY II: Fill the 'Chill Chart' with the different ways you relax to focus better in the exam hall.

Scan the QR code to share your 'CHILL CHART' with others.

MY MANTRA

4

"

Be a Warrior,
Not a Worrier!

"

Be a Warrior, Not a Worrier!

Every one of us is destined for exceptional things. Exams are just one of the challenges and opportunities that are in store for us. Overcome all challenges and shine. For tomorrow belongs to you!

Someone wrote to me during one of the 'Mann Ki Baat' programmes for exam students: 'Modiji, our students should be warriors and not worriers.' I fully agree.

Ironically, the most commonly known fear is the fear of the unknown. It is natural to be mildly concerned before exams. However, worrying all the time will not help. Being in perpetual tension cannot be in fashion. Trying to appear serious may win you sympathy but not success.

Be cheerful; there are no marks for looking worried. ☺

Why should the exam season be characterized by grim-looking students, strict parents and anxious teachers?

As children, and even now, some of the most captivating tales we hear are the life stories of brave warriors—women and men who showed exemplary courage. We always draw great inspiration from their bravery.

Take the example of Rani Laxmibai. During India's First War of Independence, when the imperialist forces were closing in, she had two choices—to be a worrier or a warrior. She did not bow down and chose instead to fight, thus being immortalized as one of the greatest freedom fighters India has ever produced!

One of my most memorable meetings was with the Indian cricket team that won the Blind T20 World Cup in 2017. Each one of the players is an inspirational warrior. Yes, they faced obstacles in life. But they fought with fortitude, against circumstances and against opponents on the field. They made the nation proud. In the same way, when it comes to exams, be a warrior and not a worrier.

Pay no attention to tension.

Write the exams bravely and the future is yours!

ACTIVITY I: How worried are you during exams? Tick the image that best describes your emotion . . .

ACTIVITY II: What are your biggest worries about exams and how do you tackle them?

_____

_____

_____

_____

_____

_____

_____

_____

_____

_____

_____

_____

_____

_____

_____

_____

 Scan the QR code to share your thoughts with others to help them deal with their worries.

MY MANTRA

5

"

Knowledge Is Permanent— **Pursue It**

"

Knowledge Is Permanent—Pursue It

The aim of learning is to gain knowledge. When knowledge is pursued, marks will automatically follow (as a by-product).

When you visit a doctor, do you ask for his or her college mark sheet? No, you trust the doctor's skills to cure you. When you go to a lawyer, you do not want to see the LLB marks of that lawyer, you rely on his or her ability to understand the case and argue it well.

Similarly, it is the knowledge and skills you acquire that will matter.

The journey of acquiring knowledge is itself a rewarding experience. It leads you to joy and does not burden you with pressure.

Focusing simply on marks not only builds undue pressure but also limits what you absorb. You will acquire selective knowledge. In case a question is asked outside what you've prepared, you might fumble.

Moreover, partial knowledge is more harmful in life than scoring low marks.

If you study to gain knowledge, no question will seem tough.

Enjoy learning for what it is, and not with any limitations.

ACTIVITY: These three personalities are known for their pursuit of knowledge. Identify them based on the clues below.

Personality 1

* He overcame multiple odds right from a very young age and pursued knowledge. He went on to study in world-renowned institutions.
* His personal library is said to have contained over 50,000 books.
* He was independent India's first Law Minister and the architect of our Constitution.

Personality 2

* Right from his childhood, he was always immersed in solving mathematical problems that were advanced for his age.
* In 1913, G.H. Hardy received a letter containing stunningly complex mathematical theorems and formulations from this person.
* In 1918, he was elected a Fellow of the Royal Society. At the age of thirty-one, he was one of the youngest to achieve this.

Personality 3

* In 1920, he took the Indian Civil Service exams in London and stood fourth. However, he rejected the lucrative job and returned to India.
* In 1930, he was elected Mayor of Calcutta.
* He famously said, 'Give me blood, and I shall give you freedom.'

Go to Page 175 for the answers.

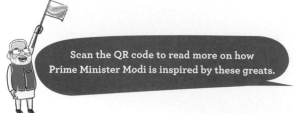

Scan the QR code to read more on how Prime Minister Modi is inspired by these greats.

6

"

Compete—
with Yourself

"

Compete—with Yourself

You are your own best competitor.

Is it not more joyful to solve a question or a problem you weren't able to earlier, than to solve one your classmate could not? **See yourself as your own competitor instead of competing with others.** Focus on enhancing your own knowledge. The key to success lies in excellence. And excellence can be achieved by expanding your own capacity until you reach your true potential.

When you are preparing, focus on your improvement areas. Ask yourself questions like:

- Do I need to work on my vocabulary?
- Am I able to solve maths problems faster than I could before?
- How can I improve my concentration?

Do you know of the famous athlete Sergey Bubka? I had mentioned him during one of the 'Mann Ki Baat' programmes. He kept bettering his own world record for the men's pole vault not once, not twice, but a record thirty-five times!

When you compete with others, there are three possible outcomes. You are better, or worse, or equal to the other person.

- If you are better, you might become overconfident.
- If you are worse, you might get frustrated.
- And in case you are equal, you might not feel the urgency to improve.

Temporary competition may damage friendships permanently. Competing with yourself makes you better.

ACTIVITY: Pick an improvement area and track your progress using this scorecard. Claim your badges along the way.

SCORECARD

WHAT DO YOU WANT TO IMPROVE IN?

_____

DATE	CURRENT LEVEL	TARGET

ACHIEVED TARGET ON: _____

CLAIM YOUR BADGE

 Scan the QR code to download more scorecards.

7

"

It's Your Time—
Make the Most of It

"

It's Your Time—Make the Most of It

Another name for time management is self-discipline. Proper time management is an effective tool for performing well in the exams.

Each day has a 'clock time' of twenty-four hours but 'effective time' varies from person to person and determines what one can achieve.

Every individual is blessed with unique abilities. These abilities are best channelled through quality time management. So, time management is nothing but ability management. It is the means to harness one's innate abilities towards enriching one's own life.

Students can chart a plan of action for their exam preparation and decide how best to utilize twenty-four hours.

Once that plan of action is prepared, follow it diligently. When a particular time is allotted for something, devote your mind and body solely to it. Initially, it may seem difficult to do so but, through persistence, following the timetable will become an integral part of your routine.

With an effective and organized schedule, you can take one thing at a time instead of thinking about everything all the time. And any possible pressure is divided. Pressure, when concentrated and accumulated, becomes tough to handle. Thus, proper time management is also proper pressure management. Looking preoccupied all the time will not help.

Remember, while planning your preparation, flexibility is essential. Plan for the important tasks but always keep some scope for dynamic changes that may arise as you go along.

Exam time is not the right time to experiment and make attempts to change your habits drastically.

Have faith in your own method and style.

ACTIVITY: Here is a sample timetable of one of the Exam Warriors.

Make your own timetable by filling up the 24-hour clock with your daily activities.

Scan the QR code and share a picture of your timetable.

MY MANTRA

8

"

The Present Is
God's Greatest
'Present'—
**Live Here
and Now**

"

The Present Is God's Greatest 'Present'—Live Here and Now

The mind often wanders back to events of the past, or to dreams about the future, perhaps even fearing the unknown. Thus, one forgets to live in the present, which is the only opportunity to make things happen.

The most important time is NOW, so make the most of it. It is not that the past or the future is unimportant. Learn from the past and plan for the future, but work in the present.

Success or setbacks from the past should not weigh us down in the present.

Focusing on the present is something I learnt to do when I held various organizational responsibilities. The magnitude of work combined with the wide range of people I had to meet taught me that such focus is the best way to do justice to both.

When I am doing something or meeting someone, I am completely immersed in it. My mind does not drift towards anything else.

To remain in the present, always keep calm. Whenever you feel agitated, take a few deep breaths and bring your thoughts in order. It is a good practice to observe one's own thoughts. This way, before our thoughts waver from the present task, we can guide our concentration back.

I will never forget what Sachin Tendulkar said to young students during one of the 'Mann Ki Baat' episodes: 'When you play cricket, do you think about the ball you faced in the past? Or the ball you will face in the future? Or do you concentrate on the ball you are about to face in that moment alone? If you keep thinking about the previous ball or the next ball, how will you hit the ball which is thrown at you now?'

ACTIVITY: What are the things on your mind at this moment?

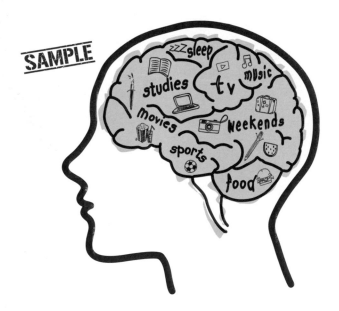

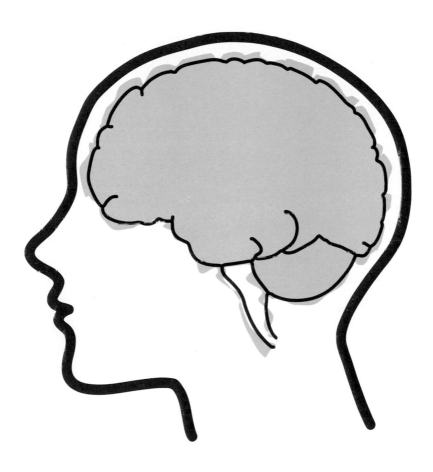

Click a picture and scan the QR code to let others know what's on your mind.

MY MANTRA

9

"

Technology Is a Great Teacher—
Embrace It

"

Technology Is a Great Teacher—Embrace It

Technology is about speed and simplicity.

It is amazing to see the way our youth connects with technology. Its impact on the education sector is extremely positive. Various learning apps, 'smart classrooms' and the online availability of rich learning material are making education fun and more accessible. Even outside the classroom, video games, PlayStations and Internet gaming are very popular among the youth.

There are some who believe that technology distracts students from their studies, particularly taking a toll on concentration. One of the raging debates on technology is about whether it is an enabler or a destructor, especially for students.

I view technology as a positive force multiplier. Personally, I have benefited tremendously from technology. I use it not only in governance but also to interact with people from across India and the world. It is a simple and an effective way to serve people.

When it comes to technology, it is essential to have a balance. **Get attracted to it, not addicted.** Use it smartly and soundly but never let technology get the better of you.

For instance, when you are spending time with parents, relatives and friends, your focus should be on people, not phones! At the dinner table, enjoy the food—your phones, iPads and video games can wait.

You may use the PlayStation but never forget the playing field. The experience of playing in the field with your friends has no substitute.

You could also try having 'tech-free time' and 'tech-free zones'—spend a certain part of the day or designate some spaces at home without any technological indulgence. This may connect you with finer aspects of life you were previously unaware of.

During meetings, I never access a mobile phone or any other gadget. Even during one-to-one meetings, my entire time is devoted to that interaction. Other things can wait.

Many people will tell you to completely stop watching television, or be off the Internet during exams. I would never suggest such a drastic measure. These aspects of technology bring a refreshing element to your otherwise fixed routine of books.

Use technology to become smart and to unwind smartly.

ACTIVITY: Have a 'No-Gadget Hour' and describe your experience.

Scan the QR code to share your experience with others.

MY MANTRA

10

"

To Do Your Best,
**Take Adequate
Rest**

"

To Do Your Best, Take Adequate Rest

Adequate rest is a must.

In between long hours of preparation, memorizing facts, practising solutions for mathematical problems and writing exams, take adequate rest.

It is as important to focus as it is to de-focus. Along with intense and continuous focus on studies, you must switch off, unwind and refresh the mind. **De-focus, for it enables better focus.**

Take a break from your studies; listen to music, read a book, practise deep breathing, relax your muscles or practise *shavasana*. Go out for a walk, play a game that you enjoy or spend some time with the family. Those who have pets could spend time with them. Outdoor activities for relaxation are strongly recommended in the run-up to exams.

Our scriptures have taught us that our body is composed of the **Panchamahabhootas**—the five elements of *Prithvi* (earth), *Jal* (water), *Vayu* (air), *Akash* (sky) and *Agni* (fire). No wonder then, that contact with even a few of these elements can be extremely rejuvenating. A shower on a tiring day, crisp sunshine on a cold day or a walk in the cool breeze—these bring us in touch with the core of our being and energize our mind and body.

In my younger days, I had a habit of spending time swimming in a lake in my village. I cherished the open skies, the cool water and the lively breeze—oneness with nature can be most refreshing.

ACTIVITY: Make your 'Take a Break' poster.

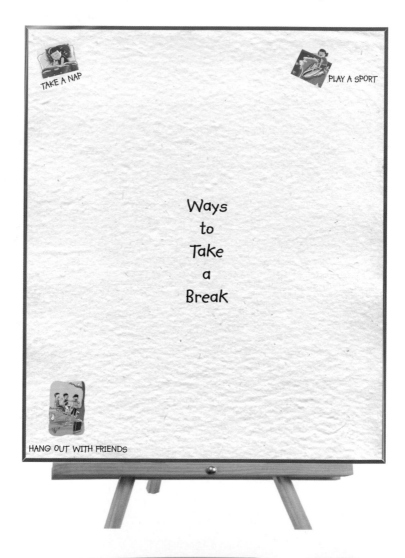

Scan the QR code to let the world know how you CHILL!

11

"

Sleep Is a Great Weapon— **Sharpen It**

"

Sleep Is a Great Weapon— Sharpen It

It may seem strange for someone to tell students to sleep during the exam season but sleep is in fact a great weapon that must be sharpened.

On many occasions people have asked me, 'Modiji, how do you manage such high energy levels through the day despite the heavy workload and perhaps even less sleep?'

I say that I remain fresh because of the good quality of sleep I get.

The quality of sleep matters. It is futile to sleep for any number of hours if that sleep is not sound.

My sleep cycle varies from four to six hours, depending on my workload. However, the hours of sleep that I get are very sound and that refreshes me for the next day. In fact, I am asleep within moments of hitting the bed, and get out of bed moments after waking up. When I go to sleep, I do not take any worries with me and when I wake up, I am ready for the new day, absolutely fresh.

My mind functions best after I have had a good rest.

A fresh mind can think and recall better than one that's desperate for a nap. Inadequate sleep can make even an easy question paper seem tough. Good sleep improves alertness and sharpens concentration.

After every exam, the best way to recharge yourself is to switch off from the world around you by taking a nap.

A good night's sleep is the key to doing well in exams. It will complement your preparation.

ACTIVITY: Rest well before the exam or stay up all night to study? What would you prefer and why?

Rest Well   ### Stay Up

Scan the QR code to let others know your preference and know their views.

12

" Play to Shine "

Play to Shine

I often say, 'जो खेले वो खिले' (Jo khele woh khile)—'One who plays, shines.'

If you devote some time to outdoor games in the midst of intense studies, it will help make your preparations more effective. Go out and play. That way, you also get a well-deserved break. In fact, even the day before an exam, a short game or a quick run can do wonders.

A unique quality of sport is the complete oneness of the player with the sport being played. No matter who is playing, young or old, rich or poor, any sport completely immerses the mind and body of a sportsperson in itself. This ability to become one with what we do helps us do great things. This also helps tremendously in exam preparations.

Outdoor sports enhance the spirit of fellowship among friends and instil the values of teamwork.

Apart from this, playing has many tangible benefits:

- You take in more oxygen.
- Your blood circulation improves.
- Your muscles loosen.
- Your mind–body coordination becomes better.
- Your concentration improves.
- Your stamina increases.

A possible feeling of saturation after long hours of studying disappears.

So, play to shine.

ACTIVITY: State your favourite sport and make a dream team of your favourite players.

PLAY TO SHINE

Sport: _____

Team Name: _____

Players: _____

1. _____
2. _____
3. _____
4. _____
5. _____
6. _____
7. _____
8. _____
9. _____
10. _____
11. _____

Scan the QR code to make customized cards for your team.

13

"

Be Your Own
Anchor—
**Celebrate Your
Strengths**

"

Be Your Own Anchor—Celebrate Your Strengths

Swami Vivekananda would often quote from the Upanishads, 'अहं ब्रह्मास्मि' (*Aham Brahmasmi*), which means, each soul is a manifestation of divinity. Meditate daily on this reality and it will fill you with an unparalleled spirit of self-confidence.

Your ability, knowledge and preparation are enough to propel you towards success. Have faith. Remember what Swamiji taught, 'If you have faith in all the Gods . . . and still have no faith in yourselves, there is no salvation for you.'

Trust yourself! During exam time, the possibility of rumours and misinformation reaching you can be high. Do not fall prey to them. **Rumours are negative, almost never true and will not affect you if you are well prepared.**

Have you observed divers? They jump into the water from a height trusting their own abilities, not with the hope that someone else will catch them.

Confidence is not about knowing everything; it comes from identifying and celebrating even the smallest of your strengths. You never know which of your many strengths can help you or others in good and not so good times. **In fact, always be proactive in serving others, for that is an excellent way to realize your own hidden strengths.**

Hence, instead of allowing your weaknesses to overpower your strengths, celebrate your strengths, put them to good use and overcome your weaknesses.

ACTIVITY: My Name—My Strengths . . . Write an attribute of yours for every letter in your name.

S:	Smart
T:	Trustworthy
U:	Understanding
D:	Dynamic
E:	Energetic
N:	Neat
T:	Team Player

Scan the QR code to share it with others.

14

"

Revise and Become Wise

"

Revise and Become Wise

Thorough revision is both necessary and helpful. It sharpens what you have learnt and also helps recall concepts systematically and easily.

In your day-to-day lives, the habit of being organized about 'small' things such as keeping your school bag, shoes and uniform in their proper places not only helps in retrieving them later but also trains the mind to be methodical. This training of the mind will help to systematically store information and retrieve it.

Whenever you are studying, identify the topics where pre-exam revision will be essential.

There are multiple ways to revise and recall concepts with ease.

Writing down the key points is a good way to revise.

Some young friends might like to use mind mapping to organize what they have learnt. Some may make attractive short forms, acronyms and formulas. Recall how you remembered the colours of the rainbow with the word 'VIBGYOR'.

Debating and discussing particular topics may be a useful tool for revision. Back in the day, when I held organizational responsibilities in my political party, we would divide ourselves into different teams (some would act like Opposition spokespersons), each of which would approach an issue through a different prism. This way, we could assess how prepared we were and also understand the areas in which we needed improvement.

At times, others can give us substantive feedback on where we are lagging behind. I have another anecdote to share, this one from my schooldays. Being part of a school play, I had to deliver a particular dialogue which, for some reason, I was struggling with. The director of the play got impatient and said he would be unable to direct me if I kept saying the dialogue in that manner.

Naturally, I thought I was doing it perfectly, so I found it perplexing that the director would say this about me. The next day, I asked him to act like me and show me what I was doing wrong. In a matter of seconds, I realized where I was going wrong and was able to improve myself.

I am told that after the day's play, sportspersons go back to the drawing board and watch clippings not only of their own game but also that of the opposing team. This helps them improve.

There are many more ways of smart revision that can be extremely helpful. Pick the ones that suit you best and keep revising, smartly and regularly.

ACTIVITY: Given on the next page is an example of a mind map. Likewise, you can make a mind map on a topic of your choice.

Scan the QR code to share your mind map with others and learn from theirs as well.

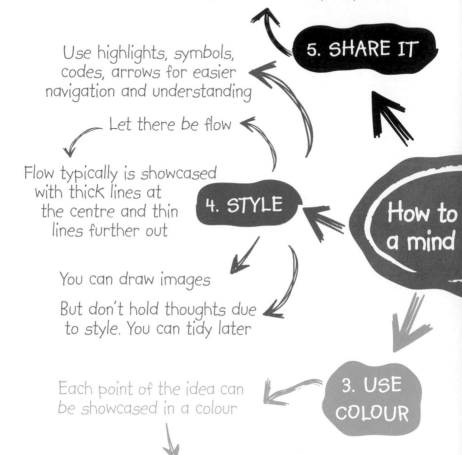

When you finish, share it with your study buddies and also see their mind maps for a fresh perspective

5. SHARE IT

Use highlights, symbols, codes, arrows for easier navigation and understanding

Let there be flow

Flow typically is showcased with thick lines at the centre and thin lines further out

4. STYLE

How to a mind

You can draw images

But don't hold thoughts due to style. You can tidy later

Each point of the idea can be showcased in a colour

3. USE COLOUR

Branches under each point can carry the same colour

Gather the information you may need along with relevant stationery

1. WRITE YOUR TOPIC/IDEA IN THE CENTRE

Use blank sheets in landscape format

Use a colourful image or symbol to represent the topic in the centre

make map

2. THINK OF THE MAIN POINTS RELATED TO THE TOPIC

Each point on the idea can become a branch of the mind map

Keywords of that topic can be used to make the branch longer

Start from the 12 o'clock position and move clockwise to write the topics

MY MANTRA

15

"

Little Things
Matter—
**Observe Exam
Discipline**

"

Little Things Matter—Observe Exam Discipline

You may have heard these things many times from many people. However, one can't speak of exams and not mention these little things that matter.

Organize yourself before the exam. To begin with, pack your exam essentials the previous evening. These include stationery, and your hall ticket and identity card among other things.

Acquainting yourself with the exam centre will help you get rid of last-minute jitters before an exam. Make it a point to arrive early. A late or delayed entry creates avoidable panic, which will affect you adversely.

Follow all the rules of the exam centre; take only permitted items inside the examination room.

Don't be in a hurry to start writing the answers. Take a minute or two to read the instructions and question paper properly.

On coming back home after the exam, make sure your hall ticket and other exam essentials are kept safely, as they will be needed again.

Exam times are nothing out of the ordinary. Stick to your normal routine, your everyday stationery—including something as minute as your regular pen—and comfortable clothes. Sticking to normality helps calm one's mind and averts unexpected surprises.

ACTIVITY: Prepare your exam checklist for ready reference. Don't forget to pin it up in your study room.

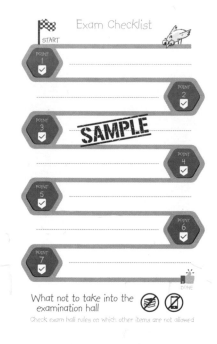

Find the tearaway Exam Checklist on Page 181.

16

"

Your Exam, Your Methods— **Choose Your Own Style**

"

Your Exam, Your Methods—
Choose Your Own Style

Have you been in a situation where, after the exam, you think: *I could have written much more, but ran out of time?* Proper time management during the exam can change this.

Just remember not to get stuck on any one question. Move to the next one. You can always come back to the unanswered question later.

Similarly, you may know an answer particularly well and may want to keep writing, but there are other questions to be answered. Write what you feel is essential in the spirit of the question, and move ahead.

Not every question will be equally simple or difficult. Some of you may prefer to answer the simpler questions first and tackle the complex ones later, while others do the opposite.

I am told some schools and boards allot an additional fifteen minutes for reading the questions. This is the ideal time for students to collect their thoughts and plan how to approach the question paper.

There is no ideal style of answering questions. Find your own unique style while keeping in mind the requirements of each question and the subject.

Always remember to double-check every question, especially where data and numbers are involved.

ACTIVITY: There are many ways to reach
'SUCCESS'. Discover them!

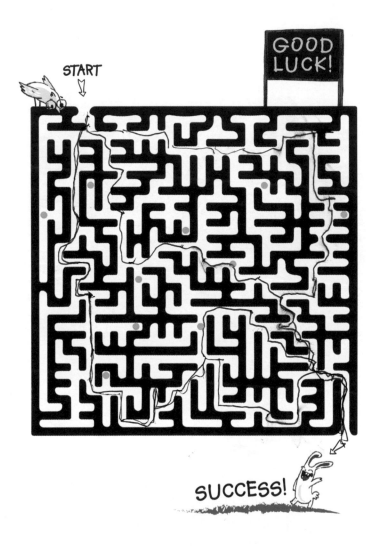

Find the solution on Page 175.

17

"

Presentation Is Key— **Master It**

"

Presentation Is Key—Master It

Quality of content is certainly of prime importance in your answers. Along with it, your presentation needs attention too.

As the Prime Minister of India, I receive numerous presentations by ministers and officials about their work. The essence of the rich content comes out even better with quality presentation.

Good presentation is like beautiful icing on your favourite cake—it enhances the taste and leaves a lasting impression.

How a student presents the answers on the answer sheet is significant. While writing an exam, give the examiner the least possible stress. An examiner always likes well-structured arguments, presented neatly and coherently.

Remember, your examiner does not know you, and therefore, he or she is not evaluating you. He or she is evaluating your answer sheet and what you have written. Proper space management, well-organized content and neat handwriting make for good presentation, which will leave a strong impact on the examiner's mind.

In that spirit, work on your presentation skills throughout the year and keep practising the art of effective articulation. Seek the help of teachers, parents and others time and again if required.

Ensure that your emphasis on presentation is not time-consuming. Make it a part of your style.

ACTIVITY: Put yourself in the examiner's chair. Grade the answers below on the basis of their presentation.

Presentation matters. The key ~~of~~ to good presentation is neatness. If we are not neat, then the answer cannot be read or ~~understand~~ understood easily. Structuring ~~the~~ an answer is important. There should be ~~stategic~~ strategic uses of points ~~and~~, headings, paragraphs, diagrams ~~&~~ and other modes of good ~~presentation~~ presentation.

Presentation matters :-

1. Neat Presentation-
   If the writing is not neat, then the answer cannot be easily read or understood.

2. Structure is important-
   Points, paragraphs, and headings make your answer look well-organised.

3. Usage of Diagrams-
   This helps illustrate your answer better.

PRESENTATION MATTERS:

The key points that can make the presentation of your answer better are:

1. _Neatness_ - If the hand-writing is not neat, then the answer cannot be easily read or understood.

2. _Structure_ - You can give a well-organised structure to your answers with the help of:
   - Points
   - Paragraphs
   - Headings

3. _Diagrams_ - They help illustrate your answer better. E.g.

MY MANTRA

18

" To Cheat Is to Be Cheap "

To Cheat Is to Be Cheap

Cheating is WRONG. This point cannot be stressed enough.

I lend my voice to all those who have previously counselled students against dishonest practices during exams.

Cheating is extremely harmful. It gives a fake sense of accomplishment and defeats the purpose of examinations. If you get caught, you might be severely punished, and if you don't, you might become a habitual cheater. Habitual cheating corrupts the soul. Why mortgage your soul and integrity for anything?

Cheating is the biggest disservice you can do to your parents, society and, most importantly, to yourself.

Instead of wasting time thinking of ways to cheat, why not work on innovative ways to study and recall important concepts?

True success is that which is achieved through hard work, and not by copying someone else's work. Success lasts only when earned.

As students, remember that dishonesty is not restricted to exams alone. Be it class assignments or projects, always focus on original work. People have lost their jobs, reputation and respect just because they plagiarised a few lines from somewhere.

Let human creativity always prevail over cheating and plagiarism.

ACTIVITY: Lend your voice to the 'No Cheating' movement by filling the pledge.

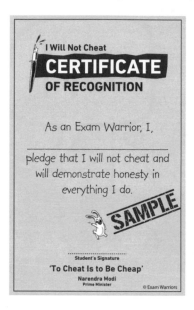

Find the tearaway 'No Cheating' Pledge on Page 183.

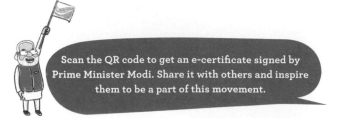

Scan the QR code to get an e-certificate signed by Prime Minister Modi. Share it with others and inspire them to be a part of this movement.

19

"

The Answer Sheet
Is a
One-Way Ticket—
Move Ahead

"

The Answer Sheet Is a One-Way Ticket— Move Ahead

Do you know the best part about any exam? It is that it lasts only for two to three hours. But rarely does an exam end in your mind immediately.

It keeps playing on your mind and you start discussing with friends, 'Was this answer right?', 'Did you answer this question or that?', 'What method did you use to solve that sum?'

It is not advisable to spend hours discussing the exam paper with family and friends. It is a colossal waste of time and energy. Often, the discussion can take a negative turn that can harm your self-confidence and ability to prepare well for the next exam.

After class tests and preparatory exams, and during other assignments, it may be helpful to spend time analysing your answer sheets to hone your strengths as well as overcome your weaknesses.

However, mid-exam worry during your board or final exams harms your mind and weakens your preparation for the next paper. It is more prudent to prepare for the next paper than to worry about the one you just wrote.

There is no point in thinking about the answers in an already submitted answer sheet. It has begun its one-way journey. **If you have answered well, you do not need to worry. In case you haven't, even then, do not worry about it because there is nothing you can do to alter it now.**

Like you have exams, I had one of my own exams—the Gujarat elections of December 2012. The day polling ended and the votes were cast, I moved ahead and began to work on the tasks at hand. I still remember going to oversee preparations for the upcoming Vibrant Gujarat Global Summit and reviewing an irrigation project. For me, the vote, like your answer sheet, was a one-way ticket.

Prepare, write, move ahead.

ACTIVITY: In the puzzle given below, search for things that you generally do (or don't) after the exam.

```
A H W D R Y T K J L P O U V R
S F O T H B H C J N J E K G I
B S R H C D I S C U S S F T K
X C R T H N U I U E M B A P T
Q G Y E F H K L N E R J I R A
M A U S R N D I O C A R C E L
I P R W A S E Y X J S V P P Q
Z N E W O Y R P L A N L A R
N M L I R I A C I N F G W R U
N Q A E N T I A L I S D G E M
Q W X K R E V I E W A S D F G
```

DO

1. PLAN
2. Relax
3. Prepare

DON'T

1. Worry
2. Discuss
3. Review

Find the solution on Page 176.

MY MANTRA

20

"

Discover Yourself— Experience All That Life Offers

"

Discover Yourself—Experience All That Life Offers

Seeing or knowing about something is good but it is incomplete. Experiencing it is altogether different, for it gives a sense of completeness. Looking at a beautiful picture of a river is one thing, but to truly know its beauty, you need to step into the waters and experience it.

Whenever you have an opportunity, seize it and explore the world around you. Make your life about new experiences. Go and travel in the general compartment of a train for twenty-four hours without a reservation. Instead of where you usually play, go to a different playground and engage with a new set of people.

Venture out and understand the problems being faced by common citizens. And then evaluate your life and challenges in that light.

Go out and work with an organization involved in community service. There's nothing more joyful and fulfilling than the satisfaction that comes from serving others and making a positive difference in society. It will ignite a spirit of service and compassion in you.

Step out of your comfort zone. Do things differently and do different things. Surprise yourself. In the process, you will get to know yourself. Spend some time in pursuit of the things you could not do because of the exams.

Pursue a new hobby like learning a musical instrument, a language or a sport.

During exams, you lived to learn . . . Now go out and learn to live.

Throw yourself at life; it is the best teacher!

ACTIVITY I: Describe interesting experiences in which you stepped out of your comfort zone and learnt from life.

_____

_____

_____

_____

_____

_____

ACTIVITY II

Suggest volunteering organizations that you know of or have worked in, which can also provide volunteering opportunities to others. Scan the QR code to share.

21

" India Is Incredible— Travel and Explore "

India Is Incredible—
Travel and Explore

Travel broadens the mind and gives you an opportunity to meet different people and experience unique cultures. Travel and discover the country after your exams.

Blessed with unparalleled beauty and diversity, India has many things to offer. The mountains, lush green forests, majestic rivers, historical monuments and forts—symbols of our rich history and traditions—tell stories in a way that you can never find in books.

I am sure there is a lot to see in your home town and state as well. Go out and explore your own place. Look out for unexplored and little-known wonders. Do not forget to share a picture with me, using #IncredibleIndia.

If you have not spent time with your family because of the exams, visit them. I remember, in my time, the moment the exams got over, children would go to their maternal uncle's home. All the cousins would get together and enjoy.

There is an interesting initiative, *Ek Bharat Shreshtha Bharat,* to celebrate the cultural vibrancy of the country and bring states closer. The initiative includes several activities which will interest you. You can go and see a friend living in another state and invite that friend to visit yours.

I had the good fortune of travelling to almost every district of India even before I became Chief Minister. I experienced first-hand how people across the length and breadth of the nation are different and yet so similar. This is truly unity in diversity.

Set out to experience India. I promise that you will enjoy it.

ACTIVITY I: Make a travel bucket list of the places you want to visit in India.

Incredible !ndia

'I urge people, especially the youth, to discover the wonders of #IncredibleIndia in the months to come.'

Narendra Modi
Prime Minister

Scan the QR code and share your #IncredibleIndia moments with others.

ACTIVITY II: Draw a rough map of your city, district or state. Mark tourist attractions which others could visit.

Scan the QR code to share it with others. Invite them to experience #IncredibleIndia.

MY MANTRA

22

" As One Journey Ends, Another Begins "

As One Journey Ends,
Another Begins

Life is an endless journey.

When your board exams end, you will find yourself on the verge of a new phase of life—one in which you will have to make various choices: of subjects, courses and colleges.

When you make those choices, remember, your passion makes for the best vocation. Your interests will shape your future.

Create your own opportunities. Be the master of your destiny. Today, there are tremendous opportunities in fields which were unimaginable even a decade ago.

Take sports, for instance. You can become a sportsperson, select sports management or journalism as your career, manufacture sports equipment or even train other athletes.

Whatever be your passion, there are multiple possibilities just waiting to be harnessed.

Trying to become someone is taking a conventional path . . . take the road less travelled.

ACTIVITY I: Describe the most memorable experiences of your school life.

- -

- -

- -

- -

- -

- -

- -

- -

- -

- -

- -

- -

- -

- -

- -

- -

Scan the QR code to share your experiences with others.

ACTIVITY II: Write a 'Talent Tip' for your friend suggesting how your friend's unique talents can make a difference to society.

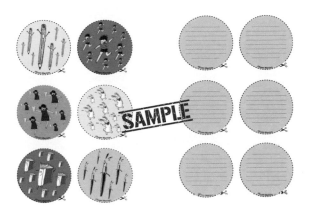

Find the tearaway 'Talent Tips' on Pages 185–88.

 Scan the QR code to share 'TALENT TIPS' with more friends.

MY MANTRA

23

"

Aspire,
Not to Be,
but to Do

"

Aspire, Not to Be, but to Do

People often ask me, 'Modiji, when you were young, did you ever dream of becoming the Prime Minister of the world's largest democracy?'

I must confess, forget dreaming about becoming the Prime Minister, I was never even a class monitor!

All my life I have lived by a simple mantra—'कुछ बनने के नहीं, कुछ करने के सपने देखो!' (Kuch banne ke nahi, kuch karne ke sapne dekho)—Aspire not to become something but to do something.

'Aspiring to do something' leads you, 'Aspiring to become something' misleads you. Normally, the desire to become something is driven by the expectations of the family, fashionable professional trends, peer pressure or fantasies of fame, money and power. It distances you from your true potential and gradually snuffs out the innate passion you are blessed with.

However, the desire to do something, which is invariably fuelled by your natural instincts, will lead you to your true destiny.

Do not merely dream of becoming a doctor, engineer or lawyer. **Think of how best you can make a difference to society and let that ideal guide you.**

ACTIVITY: If there was no restriction on resources or opportunities, what would you do for society and why?

Scan the QR code to let others know.

24

"

Be Grateful

"

Be Grateful

Your success is not yours alone. Behind your success are the efforts of many people whom you meet (and don't meet) in your daily life.

Your parents are giving their all so that you can lead a comfortable life.

Your siblings are the strongest source of support for you.

Your teachers are giving you a wonderful education that opens multiple windows of opportunity. Teaching is among the noblest professions in society. A teacher not only nurtures a student but also builds a nation.

Think of the support staff in your school, the tailor who stitches your uniform, the bookstore from where you purchase your textbooks, notebooks and stationery.

Remember the bus driver and conductor who bring you to school and take you back home every day. If you study in a residential school, remember the cooks who ensure you are well-fed.

You would not have reached where you are without their help, support and blessings.

Think also of those countless people whom you've never met but who play a vital role in your life—the farmer who produces the food you enjoy and the labourer who built your school brick by brick to give you a place to study.

These unsung heroes are the makers of India and we must be grateful to them.

ACTIVITY I: Because they are . . . you are. Who are the people you are grateful to?

NAME	WHO THEY ARE

ACTIVITY II: Write 'Gratitude Cards' for those whom you are grateful to. Present the cards to them and make them feel special.

A BIG THANK YOU

To.....................................

SAMPLE

from
....

Find the tearaway 'Gratitude Cards' on Pages 189–94.

Click pictures while presenting the 'GRATITUDE CARDS' and scan the QR code to upload.

MY MANTRA

25

> "
>
> Yoga Brings
> Transformation—
> **Practise
> Regularly**
>
> "

Yoga Brings Transformation—
Practise Regularly

Many people will tell you that yoga-pranayama is not for youngsters but for when you are older.

This is far from the truth.

Practising yoga with full awareness in one's youth is the most effective way to achieve holistic development of the self.

Yoga brings good health and happiness, and makes the mind hassle-free. This augurs well for the exam season.

Devote some time each day, preferably in the morning, to practise yoga.

Yoga strengthens the brain and the nervous system. This sharpens the mind and improves blood circulation. Some of the balancing asanas even enhance confidence.

When one practises the various asanas and pranayama, the ability to concentrate improves. Better concentration brings about greater efficiency in learning, which in turn enhances recall power.

The overall impact is that memory, concentration and confidence are boosted. As Exam Warriors, these are the three things you will need the most. Yoga helps you with all three!

With yoga, Exam Warriors will be better prepared with their studies and more confident about life.

That yoga promotes physical fitness is well known. Along with that, yoga builds mental strength and intellectual sharpness. Regular practice of it will ensure that your mind does not waver. You will become a calmer person, less prone to panic.

Yoga deepens the connect of an individual with society and thus improves one's emotional quotient (EQ).

At the same time, yoga is a means to attaining spiritual bliss. It ignites the quest to know oneself.

Personally, yoga is integral to my daily routine. My day begins with yoga. It has helped me navigate many challenges.

Yoga is India's gift to the world. In recent times, it has been attaining immense popularity on the global stage. Since 2015, the world has been observing International Day of Yoga on a grand scale on 21 June every year. This is an extremely positive sign.

In this book, I have put together a number of asanas which will help students in exams and in life. They are easy to understand and practise.

Make yoga a part of your lives and see the change it brings!

ACTIVITY: The following pages contain information on many asanas. Practise them.

Scan the QR code to share your yoga pictures with others.

Letters to Parents and Teachers

Dear Parents,

Family is the strongest support system for any child, more so as he or she prepares for examinations. I do understand that these are crucial times, for both the student and his or her family. During this time, if there is anybody whose encouragement will make your children happy, it is you.

Keep doing everything that you can to support your children. This includes lightening the child's mood and ensuring he or she appears for the exam in a happy and stress-free manner.

You are your child's best mentor. You know your child better than anyone else, having seen him or her grow up in front of your eyes. Thus, I would request you: **always accept rather than expect.** The burden of expectations is even heavier than the school bag, and there's no point in weighing your children down with it. Ask yourself: Are you burdening your child with unreasonable expectations?

Sometimes, parents seek to realize their own unfulfilled desires through their children. In the process, the child loses a happy childhood and the parents miss out on the joy of seeing their child grow up and blossom in front of their eyes. The dreams, aspirations and ambitions of children can differ from those of their parents. Accept this and give your children the space to pursue their own dreams.

As parents, you always want the best for your child, including good schooling and a comfortable lifestyle. But one of the best gifts that you can give your child is a spirit of adventure, which will inspire your child to do something new and different. In this book too I have told my young friends to step out of their comfort zone. Comfort weakens the mind and the body. Adventure prepares one to face life's challenges and that too with poise and determination.

Spend quality time with your child. The exam season is naturally characterized by a scramble for time. Make the most of every moment you spend with your child. Remain positive and laugh. ☺

Always listen to what your child has to say. Those children who are not heard can never become good listeners and learners themselves.

Once the board exams are over, children are required to choose their subjects, colleges and universities. Guide your child to make those decisions based on his or her interests and strengths. As I have said in the book, there are several opportunities waiting to be created and harnessed. Let there be no limitations or pressure on the children.

My best wishes to you as you extend invaluable support to our young and valorous Exam Warriors.

Yours,

Narendra Modi
26 January 2018

Dear Teachers,

Let me begin by congratulating you on the wonderful work you are doing to mould and educate young minds. You belong to the noblest profession in our society and your hard work lays the foundation for a better tomorrow.

The relationship between a teacher and a student is special. Students look up to their teachers, and would not disobey them. That is why I am writing to you and seeking your support to communicate some of the ideas in this book to your students.

Needless to say, as teachers, you are vital to this effort of encouraging and supporting our Exam Warriors.

As the exams approach, some students may become nervous and develop cold feet. I am sure you will go out of your way to help them overcome their anxieties.

Every student is unique and blessed with various strengths. Your role is that of a facilitator who brings out the best in your students. Teach your students not only what is in the textbooks but also beyond. Enable them to be original and rooted thinkers who are blessed with a thirst for knowledge, a spirit of inquiry and a zeal for innovation.

It is understandable for students and parents to be thinking about college and career choices after the exams. It is heartening to note that more and more schools are institutionalizing practices of mentoring, where faculty members guide students based on the many opportunities available, in tune with their aptitude. Teachers are also helping them identify the institutions for higher studies best suited to their interests.

I hope you empower your students to pursue their interests as well as create their own opportunities. Motivate them so that they do something driven by their passion instead of seeking to become something. Today's world has numerous opportunities for the youth, which they must harness.

I also request you to keep discussing with your students how they can sit for exams in a tension-free manner, without being burdened by pressure, and how they should always pursue knowledge and not marks . . . issues that I have also tried to address in this book.

My best wishes in your continued quest to educate young minds!

Yours,

Narendra Modi
26 January 2018

Yogasanas

Prayer

ॐ असतो मा सद्गमय।
तमसो मा ज्योतिर्गमय।।
मृत्योर्मा अमृतं गमय।
ॐ शांतिः शांतिः शांतिः।।

Um asatomaa sad gamaya |
Tamasomaa jyotir gamaya |
Mrutyor maa amrtam gamaya |
Om shaantih shaantih shaantih ||

Lead me from the unreal to the real
Lead me from darkness to light
Lead me from mortality to immortality
May there be peace, peace, peace

Before you begin practising the various asanas, it is advised that you warm up and do stretching exercises for approximately 10–15 minutes. This will prepare you for yoga, improve blood circulation and make your body flexible.

SURYANAMASKARA (SUN SALUTATION)

Name

Surya or the sun is a source of energy for all living beings on earth. Suryanamaskara is a set of seven yogic poses performed in twelve steps early in the morning to refresh the mind and energize the body for the day ahead.

Technique

Starting position: Stand upright with feet together and arms by the side of the body; balance the body equally on both feet (Samasthiti).

1. **Namaskarasana:** Inhale, bring the palms in front of the chest and join them together as in Namaskara Mudra or prayer position, exhale.

2. **Hastottanasana:** Inhaling, raise both arms up keeping them close to the ears. Stretch the body as much as possible and bend backwards without bending the knees.

3. **Padahastasana:** Breathing out, bend forward from the waist, keeping the spine erect. Place the hands on the floor on either side of the feet. Try to touch the knees with the forehead.

4. **Ashwasanchalanasana:** Breathing in, place the right leg as far back as possible and bring the right knee to the floor. Bend the left leg at the knee and keep the left foot on the floor between the palms, making a 90-degree angle. Arch the spine back and look up.

5. **Santolanasana:** Stretch your left leg behind such that it is in line with your right leg, while exhaling. Your hands should align with your shoulders and your shoulders, back and hips should be in a straight line. Breathe normally when you are in this posture.

6. **Sashtanga Namaskarasana:** Exhaling slowly, gently bring the limbs of the body, toes, knees, palms, the chest and the forehead down to the floor. Lift the hips slightly, arms bending, while elbows point upwards.

7. **Bhujangasana:** Lower the hips and inhale. Raise the head and push the chest up. Raise the torso up to the navel with the spine arched back. Keep the palms on the ground and bend backwards.

8. **Parvatasana:** Breathing out, lift the hips up and lower the head and chest downwards in an 'inverted V' posture. Keep the head between the arms and the feet on the ground.

9. **Ashwasanchalanasana:** Breathing in, bend the right leg and bring it forward. Keep the right foot on the ground between the arms and the left leg stretched behind with the knee touching the ground. Arch the spine and look up.

10. **Padahastasana:** Breathing out, bring the left leg forward and place the left foot beside the right foot. Place both the palms beside the feet on the ground with the head touching the knees.

11. **Hastottanasana:** Breathing in, raise the arms and the torso. Place the arms straight above the head and bend backwards as much as possible.

12. **Namaskarasana:** Breathing out, come back to the original position. Slowly bring the arms down and join the palms in front of the chest in Namaskara Mudra or the prayer position.

This is the first cycle of one round. To complete one round of Suryanamaskara, repeat the same twelve steps and use the other leg in Ashwasanchalanasana.

Benefits
- Suryanamaskara is considered a complete yoga practice as it is the combination of various yogic elements like asana, *bandha*, mudra and so on.
- It helps to increase flexibility, lung capacity, strength and endurance, and keeps your spine in good shape.
- The regular practice of Suryanamaskara improves concentration and helps increase the height of growing children.

Caution
Avoid if you have a spinal injury; practise it as per your need and capacity.

TADASANA (PALM TREE POSE)

Name
Tadasana is often referred to as the 'palm tree pose' as the body takes the shape of a palm tree in the final position of this asana.

Technique
Starting position: Stand erect with the feet 2 inches apart and the arms by the sides of the body. Keep the head straight.

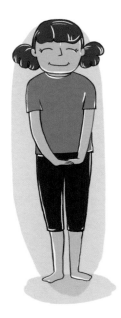

- Interlock the fingers, turn the palms outwards and inhale. Raise the arms upwards, stretch the body up and bring it in a straight line with the arms.
- Look straight ahead, raise the heels and balance the body on the toes. Hold the pose for a few seconds. Breathe normally.
- Exhale, bring the heels and the hands down. Release the fingers and come back to the starting position.

Benefits
It helps to improve concentration and removes lethargy.

Caution
Avoid doing this asana if you experience a reeling sensation or if you have a knee or ankle injury.

VRIKSHASANA (TREE POSE)

Name
Vriksha means 'tree'. In the final position of this asana, the body takes the shape of a tree. Hence it is named Vrikshasana.

Technique
Starting position: Stand erect with the feet together, arms by the sides of the body. Keep the head straight.

- Exhaling, *bend the left leg and place the left foot as high as possible on the right thigh. The heel of the left foot should touch the inner side of the right thigh.

- Balance on one foot. Inhale and raise both the arms above the head, keeping them straight. Join the palms together.
- Stay in this position for a few seconds while breathing normally.
- Exhale, bring the left foot down and place arms by the sides of the body to get back to the original position.
- Relax and repeat the procedure with the right foot on the left thigh.

Benefits
It helps to improve concentration and leads to neuromuscular coordination.

Caution
Avoid this asana if you are obese or have vertigo.

PADAHASTASANA (HANDS-TO-FEET POSE)

Name
Padahastasana is referred to as the hands-to-feet pose because in the final position of this asana, the hands are lowered and placed beside the feet.

Technique
Starting position: Stand straight with the feet together and arms by the sides of the body.

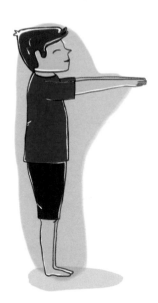

- Inhale, slowly raise the arms over the head and stretch the body upwards from the waist.
- Exhale and bend forward from the waist without arching the back.

- Place the palms on the ground *beside* the feet. Maintain this position for a few *seconds*.
- Inhale, and *slowly* come back to the standing position with the arms above the head.
- Exhale, and *bring* the arms down to the sides of the body.

Benefits
It helps to make the spine flexible, and improves digestion and memory.

Caution
This asana should be avoided if you have pain in your lower back or spinal injury.

PADMASANA (LOTUS POSE)

Name

Padma means 'lotus'. As the body takes the shape of a lotus in the final position of this asana, it is called Padmasana.

Technique

Starting position: Sit on the ground with the legs stretched in front and the spine erect.

- Fold the legs, place the left foot on the right thigh and the right foot on the left thigh. The knees should touch the ground.
- Place the hands in Jnana or Chin Mudra on the knees.

- Keep the neck and back straight.
- Close the eyes and keep the body relaxed.

Benefits

Padmasana helps to induce calmness and tranquillity. It also improves concentration and enhances memory.

Caution

If you have knee or ankle injuries, you should avoid this asana.

VAJRASANA (DIAMOND POSE)

Name
Vajrasana is a meditative asana. Its regular practice makes one sturdy and strong, which is why it is also referred to as the 'diamond pose'.

Technique
Starting position: Sit on the floor in the kneeling position with the big toes joined together.

- Position the buttocks in the space between the heels and place palms on the knees.
- The spine should be erect. Breathe normally.

Benefits

This asana is good for digestion. It also improves concentration.

Caution

If you have knee or ankle injuries, you should avoid this asana.

GOMUKHASANA (COW'S FACE POSE)

Name
Gomukhasana is also called the 'cow's face pose' as the knees, thighs and calves together make a shape that resembles a cow's face.

Technique
Starting position: Sit erect with the legs stretched.

- Fold the left leg by the side of the right hip and fold the right leg by the side of the left hip.
- Bring the left arm over the left shoulder and the right arm behind the back.
- Interlock the fingers of both hands at the back and hold for a few seconds while breathing normally.
- Repeat, changing the position of the legs and hands.

Benefits
This asana improves lung capacity and concentration, and induces inner calmness. It corrects postural deformities like drooping shoulders.

Caution
Avoid this asana if you have joint injuries or piles.

ARDHA MATSYENDRASANA
(HALF-MATSYENDRA POSE OR HALF-SPINAL TWIST POSE)

Name

Matsyendrasana is named after Yogi Matsyendranatha of Nathparampara. The full version of this asana is difficult for a beginner to master. Therefore, a modified version of the asana, called Ardha Matsyendrasana, is presented here.

The name Ardha Matsyendrasana comes from the words *ardha* meaning 'half', *matsya* meaning 'fish', Indra meaning 'King', and asana meaning 'posture' or 'seat'. It literally means the half-twisted posture of the King of fish.

Technique

Starting position: Sit on the floor with your legs stretched in front of you. Keep your back straight and legs together.

- Place your left foot beside the right knee.
- Fold the right leg and place the heel beside the left side of the hip. Place the right hand on the left knee.
- Twist your torso, shoulders and neck to look over your left shoulder.
- Hold this position while keeping the spine erect and breathing normally.
- Repeat the process with the other leg.

Benefits
- The practice of Ardha Matsyendrasana makes the spine flexible and supple, and helps to increase lung capacity.
- It helps to improve the function of the adrenal glands, liver, spleen and kidneys.
- It is the best asana for the prevention of non-communicable diseases.

Caution
Perform this asana under the supervision of a yoga expert to avoid any back or spine injury. Girls can avoid this posture during menstruation.

MAKARASANA (CROCODILE POSE)

Name
Makarasana is a relaxing posture. In this asana, the body resembles a resting crocodile and hence it is also referred to as the 'crocodile pose'.

Technique
Starting position: Lie down in the prone position (a position of the body where you lie face down).

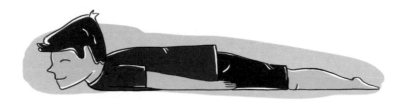

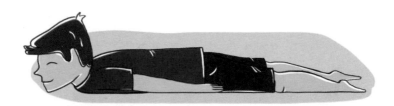

- Keep the legs apart so that the heels face each other.
- Fold the arms and place them beneath the forehead, one hand on top of the other.
- Close the eyes and relax. Hold the position for 20–30 seconds or as long as it is comfortable.

Benefits

Makarasana removes mental and physical fatigue, and helps in relieving asthma, cervical spondylosis and sciatica.

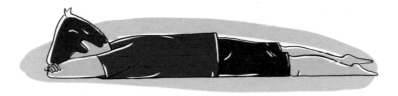

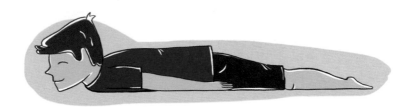

BHUJANGASANA (SERPENT POSE)

Name
Bhujangasana is also referred to as the 'serpent pose' because the final position of this asana resembles a cobra with its hood extended.

Technique
Starting position: Lie down in the prone position, then join the feet and place both hands under the shoulders with the elbows pointing upwards by the waist.

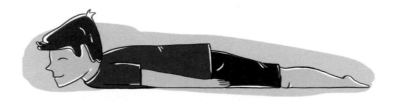

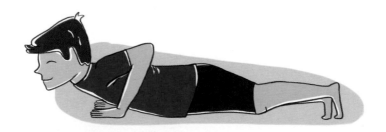

- Inhale and raise the upper body up to the navel.
- Hold the position for a short period of time while breathing normally.
- Exhale and come back to the original position. Relax in Makarasana.

Benefits
This asana improves concentration, strengthens the digestive and urinary systems and alleviates back pain while making the spine supple.

Caution
This asana is strictly prohibited for people with a hernia, intestinal tuberculosis and abdominal injuries.

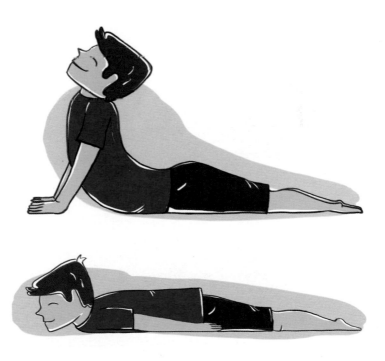

DHANURASANA (BOW POSE)

Name
Dhanurasana is also called the 'bow pose' as in the final posture of this asana, the body looks like a bow with the limbs resembling its string.

Technique
Starting position: Lie down in the prone position with the legs together and the arms beside the body.

- Exhale and hold the ankles with the hands.
- Inhaling, lift the thighs, head and chest as high as possible, balancing on the lower abdomen. Hold the position for 10–20 seconds.
- Exhale and come back to the original position. Relax in Makarasana.

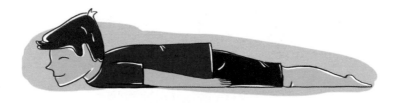

Benefits

This asana regulates the functioning of the adrenal and thyroid glands, and also of the digestive and excretory systems. It strengthens the joints of the shoulders, the spine, knees and ankles and removes stiffness in these.

Caution

If you have a hernia, peptic ulcers, colitis or appendicitis, you should not perform this asana.

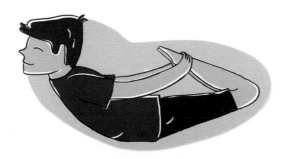

PAVANAMUKTASANA (WIND-RELIEVING POSE)

Name

As the name suggests, this asana helps in releasing trapped wind from the stomach and intestines.

Technique

Starting position: Lie down in the supine position (a position of the body where you lie face up) with the legs together, arms beside the body and palms resting on the floor.

- Inhale and bend the legs, bring the knees towards the chest.
- Encircle the knees with both arms and hold tightly.
- Exhale, and raise the head, bring the chin towards the knees and try to touch them.

- Maintain the position comfortably for 10–20 seconds.
- Release the arms, unfold the legs and place them on the floor to return to the original position.
- Relax with the legs together on the floor and the hands beside the body.

Benefits
It helps in eliminating toxic gases from the stomach and intestines, improves digestion and works to dissolve extra fat deposited in the abdominal area.

Caution
In case of abdominal injuries and severe back pain, this asana should be avoided.

CHAKRASANA (WHEEL POSE)

Name
Chakrasana is so named because the body takes the shape of a wheel in the final position of this asana.

Technique
Starting position: Lie down in the supine position.

- Bend the legs at the knees and bring the heels close to the buttocks.
- Raise the arms, place the palms on the floor beside the head with fingers pointing towards the shoulders.
- Inhale, raise the body on the arms and feet, and arch your back. Now, gently bring the head down.
- Maintain this position while breathing normally.
- Exhale, come back to the original position and relax.

Benefits

It removes stiffness from the body, makes the spine flexible and improves digestion.

Caution

This asana should be avoided in cases of weak wrists, high blood pressure, hernia and abdominal problems.

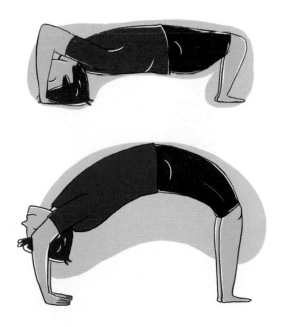

SARVANGASANA (SHOULDER STAND)

Name
It is often referred to as the 'queen of asanas'. *Sarva* means 'all', *anga* means 'limbs' or 'parts of the body' and asana means 'posture', 'position' or 'seat'. Thus Sarvangasana literally translates into 'supported-all-limbs-pose'. As the name suggests, Sarvangasana is beneficial for the entire body.

Technique
Starting position: Lie down in the supine position with the legs together, hands by the side and palms facing the floor.

- Inhale slowly and raise both legs together at a 90-degree angle to the floor.
- Now press the palms and bring the legs towards the head, so that the buttocks face upwards. Bend the elbows and support the back with the palms.

- Now bring the legs upwards till the legs, abdomen and chest form a straight line. The chin should be placed against the jugular notch.
- Hold this for some time, breathing normally.
- While coming back to the original position, first lower the buttocks, release the hands slowly and bring the legs down without raising the head.
- Relax in Shavasana.

Benefits

Sarvangasana stimulates the thyroid and parathyroid glands and normalizes their functioning. It also helps in dealing with constipation, indigestion and varicose veins. This is a beneficial asana for a growing child.

Caution

One should avoid this asana during pregnancy and menstruation, or if one suffers from high blood pressure, heart ailments, slipped disc, spondylosis, neck pain and acute thyroid problems.

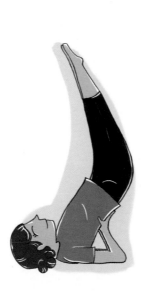 

SHAVASANA

Name
This is a relaxing posture. In this asana, the body looks still like a corpse or *shava*, which explains the name.

Technique
Starting position: Lie down in the supine position.

- Keep the feet 2-3 feet apart with the toes pointed outwards.
- Place the hands about 6 inches away from the body. Keep the fingers relaxed.
- Keep the head in a straight, comfortable position.
- Gently close the eyes and be aware of your breathing.

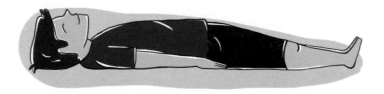

Benefits

It relaxes the body and the mind, eliminates physical and mental fatigue and boosts energy levels.

Caution

Avoid this asana if you suffer from depression or low blood pressure.

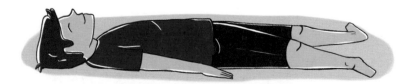

NADI SHODHANA PRANAYAMA

Name

Nadi means a 'subtle energy channel' while *shodhan* means 'purification'. Nadi Shodhana Pranayama is also known as Anulom Vilom Pranayama.

Technique

Starting position: Sit in a comfortable meditative posture, with the hands in Jnana Mudra.

- Adopt Nasagramudra with the right hand and place it on the nostrils. Close the right nostril and inhale through the left.
- Close the left nostril and exhale through the right; now inhale through the right nostril and slowly exhale through the left. This is one round of Anulom Vilom.
- Repeat four times.

Benefits

It reduces anxiety and improves concentration, and balances the right and left hemispheres of the brain.

Caution

In cases of cardiac problems and hypertension, this pranayama should be performed without the retention of breath.

SHEETALI PRANAYAMA

Name
The word Sheetali originates from the word *sheetal* which means 'cold' or 'soothing'. As the name suggests, Sheetali Pranayama cools down the body and mind.

Technique
Starting position: Sit comfortably in a meditative posture, keep both hands on the knees.

- Now bring the tongue all the way out and fold both sides of it like a tube or a straw.
- Inhale deeply through the tube formed by folding both sides of the tongue.
- After inhalation, close the mouth and exhale with both nostrils. This is one round.
- Repeat five times.

Benefits
It calms the mind and removes excess heat in the body, and is an effective stress buster.

Caution
Avoid this asana if you have low blood pressure, asthma, cold, cough or other respiratory problems.

BHRAMARI PRANAYAMA

Name
While doing this pranayama, the buzzing sound of a humming bee is produced through the nostrils. Hence it is called Bhramari.

Technique
Starting position: Sit in a comfortable meditative posture and close your eyes.

- Inhale deeply through the nose.
- Now close both the ears with the thumbs; eyes with the index fingers; nose with the middle fingers; and mouth by placing the ring fingers just above the upper lip and little fingers just below the lower lip.
- Exhale, making the deep sound of a humming bee. Concentrate on the sound. After exhalation, bring the hands back to the knees.
- This is one round. Repeat five times.

Benefits
It helps to improve concentration and relieves anxiety, anger and hyperactivity. The sound resonating in the brain creates a soothing effect on the mind and nervous system.

Caution
If you have an ear or nose infection, avoid this pranayama.

KAPALABHATI KRIYA

Name

Kapalabhati is a breathing technique for the purification of the head and the lungs. It is practised as pranayama as well as a Kriya. In Sanskrit, *kapala* means 'skull' and *bhati* means 'to shine'. Thus Kapalabhati can be literally translated as a 'skull-shining' or 'skull-cleaning' exercise.

Technique

Starting position: Sit comfortably in Padmasana.

- Rest your hands on your knees or lower belly. Breathe normally for some time.
- In a quick motion, contract your abdominal muscles and forcefully exhale all the air from your lungs.
- Allow your lungs to fill without effort. Repeat this cycle.
- Allow your breathing to return to normal.

Benefits

- It helps to balance and strengthen the nervous system, and to cleanse the respiratory tract.
- It helps to increase concentration and reduces stress, tension and anxiety.

Caution

This kriya is not advisable for patients suffering from heart disease, high blood pressure, slipped disc and spondylosis. Avoid doing it if you have a fever or headache, and abdominal pain, respiratory injury or nosebleeds.

DHYANA

Name
Dhyana refers to an act of contemplation. It pacifies the agitated mind and relaxes it. There are several techniques of meditation, but all of them have the common goal of attaining a higher level of awareness.

Technique
Starting position: Sit in a comfortable meditative posture. Keep the spine erect. Place the hands on the thighs in Jnana Mudra.

- Gently close the eyes and raise the face slightly. Breathe normally.
- Focus attention on your breath while breathing normally.
- Now, focus your attention on the space between the eyebrows. Stay in this state for five minutes or as long as possible.
- Bring your attention back to your breathing and then to the external surroundings in order to come back to the original state.

Benefits
Dhyana rejuvenates the body and mind, and helps to improve concentration. It aids behavioural modification which is the main objective of the practice of yoga.

Answers

Answers

Mantra 5

Personality 1:
Dr B.R. Ambedkar

Personality 2:
Srinivasa Ramanujan

Personality 3:
Netaji Subhas
Chandra Bose

Mantra 16

Mantra 19

```
A H W D R Y T K J L P O U V R
S F O T H B H C J N J E K G I
B S R H C D I S C U S S F T K
X C R T H N U I U E M B A P T
Q G Y E F H K L N E R J I R A
M A U S R N D I O C A R C E L
I P R W A S E Y X J S V P P Q
Z N E W O Y R P L A N L A R
N M L I R I A C I N F G W R U
N Q A E N T I A L I S D G E M
Q W X K R E V I E W A S D F G
```

Tearaways

Dear _____

Here are three things about you
that make me laugh! 😊 😄 😊

1. _____

2. _____

3. _____

Wishing you best of luck for the
exams!

© Exam Warriors

179

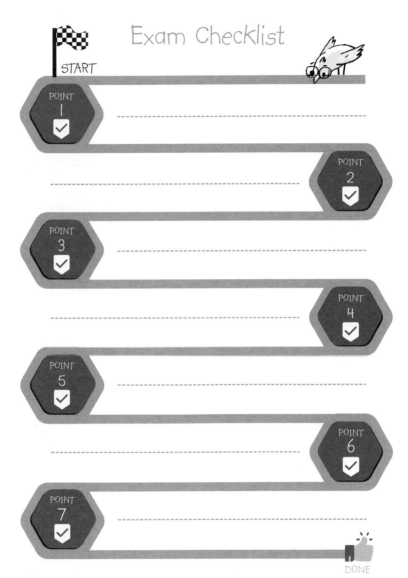

Exam Checklist

START

POINT 1

POINT 2

POINT 3

POINT 4

POINT 5

POINT 6

POINT 7

DONE

What not to take into the examination hall

Check exam hall rules on which other items are not allowed

I Will Not Cheat

CERTIFICATE

OF RECOGNITION

As an Exam Warrior, I,

_____

pledge that I will not cheat and will demonstrate honesty in everything I do.

Student's Signature

'To Cheat Is to Be Cheap'

Narendra Modi
Prime Minister

© Exam Warriors

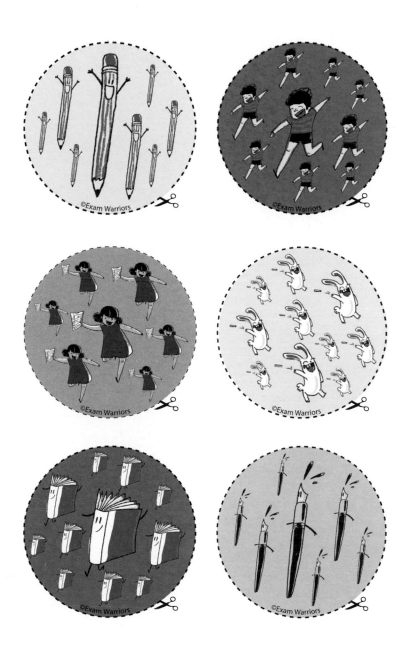

©Exam Warriors

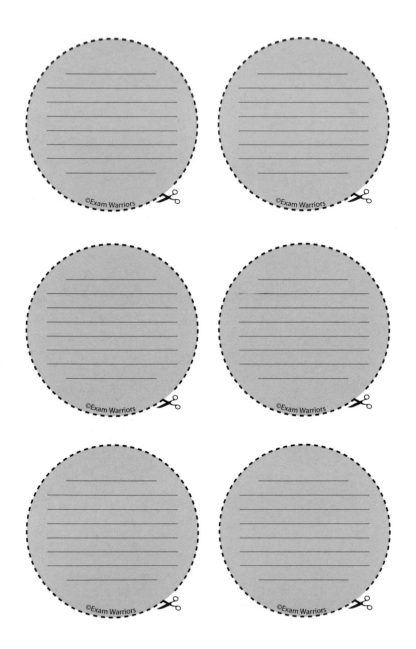

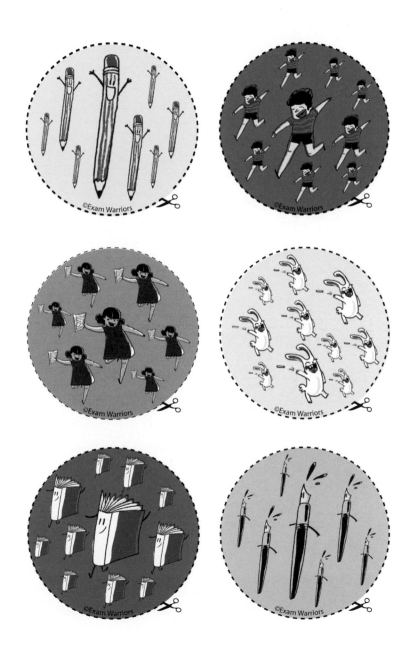

©Exam Warriors

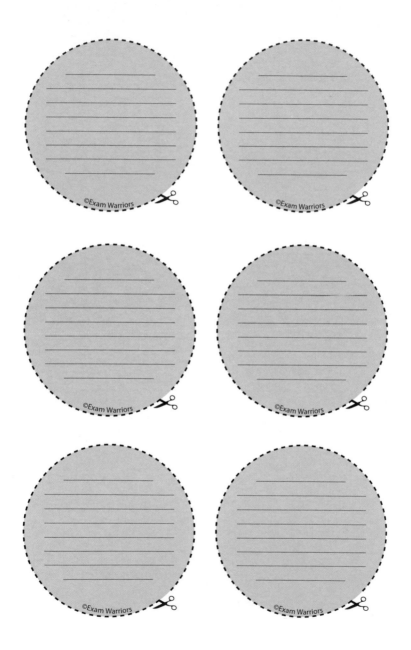

©Exam Warriors

©Exam Warriors

©Exam Warriors

©Exam Warriors

©Exam Warriors

©Exam Warriors

A BIG THANK YOU

To_____

_____

_____

_____

_____

_____

_____

_____

_____

_____

_____

_____

_____

_____

from

_____

A BIG THANK YOU

To _____

_____

_____

_____

_____

_____

_____

_____

_____

_____

_____

_____

from

_____

© Exam Warriors

A BIG THANK YOU

To _ _ _ _ _ _ _ _ _ _ _ _ _ _

_ _ _ _ _ _ _ _ _ _ _ _ _ _ _ _ _

_ _ _ _ _ _ _ _ _ _ _ _ _ _ _ _ _

_ _ _ _ _ _ _ _ _ _ _ _ _ _ _ _ _

_ _ _ _ _ _ _ _ _ _ _ _ _ _ _ _ _

_ _ _ _ _ _ _ _ _ _ _ _ _ _ _ _ _

_ _ _ _ _ _ _ _ _ _ _ _ _ _ _ _ _

_ _ _ _ _ _ _ _ _ _ _ _ _ _ _ _ _

_ _ _ _ _ _ _ _ _ _ _ _ _ _ _ _ _

_ _ _ _ _ _ _ _ _ _ _ _ _ _ _ _ _

_ _ _ _ _ _ _ _ _ _ _ _ _ _ _ _ _

_ _ _ _ _ _ _ _ _ _ _ _ _ _ _ _

from

_ _ _ _ _ _ _ _ _ _